RISKY BUSINESS

Wildlife Special Agent

Protecting Endangered Species

By

E D W A R D   R.   R I C C I U T I

*Photographs by Stephen Carpenteri
and Bruce Glassman*

A   B L A C K B I R C H   P R E S S   B O O K

W O O D B R I D G E , C O N N E C T I C U T

Published by Blackbirch Press, Inc.
260 Amity Road
Woodbridge, CT 06525

Printed in the United States

10 9 8 7 6 5 4 3 2

Library of Congress Cataloging-in-Publication Data

Ricciuti, Edward R.
    Wildlife special agent/by Edward R. Ricciuti.
       p.   cm. — (Risky business)
    Includes bibliographical references and index.
    Summary: Profiles the career of a special agent for the
Division of Law Enforcement of the Fish and Wildlife Service
while highlighting the excitement and danger involved in the
work.
    ISBN 1-56711-160-2 (lib. bdg. : alk. paper)
    1. Moulton, Richard—Juvenile literature. 2. Undercover
wildlife agents—United States—Biography—Juvenile literature.
3. U.S. Fish and Wildlife Service—Officials and employees—
Biography—Juvenile literature. 4. Wildlife management—United
States—Juvenile literature. [1. Moulton, Richard. 2. Detectives.
3. U.S. Fish and Wildlife Service. 4. Wildlife management.]
I. Title. II. Series: Risky business (Woodbridge, Conn.)
SK354.M68R535   1997
363.2'8—dc20
[B]   95-48143
                                               CIP
                                              AC

INTRODUCTION

It was a cold, rainy night at Bradley International Airport near Hartford, Connecticut. Two men walked across a parking lot to a waiting car. One of the men, who called himself "Rick Moore," carried a large box. The other man, whom we will call "John," had just brought the box by air from Africa.

When the men arrived at their car, Rick put the box down and stepped away. In the blink of an eye, he disappeared into the darkness. Suddenly, two other cars pulled up. Four men jumped out, badges held high and guns pointed. As they surrounded "John," one of them barked, "Federal agents. You're under arrest. Put your hands behind your back."

The reason for "John's" arrest was in the heavy box. Hidden inside it, under some African carvings, was a horn from a black rhinoceros, an endangered species. It is against the law to possess endangered animals or even parts of them. Smuggling—or sneaking— them into the country is also a crime.

"John" broke the law and took a chance because, ounce for ounce, rhino horn is as valuable as gold. In Asia, many people believe that ground-up rhino horn is a very powerful medicine. They are willing to pay thousands of dollars for even a small amount of it. Because of this, many rhinos have been killed for their horns and they have almost vanished from the wild.

Rick had told "John" that he wanted to buy the horn so he could later resell it for

The horn of an endangered black rhino can bring a great deal of money in illegal trade.

a big profit. However, Rick had not told "John" the truth, not even about his name. Rick's real name is Richard ("Rich") Moulton, and he is a Special Agent for the Division of Law Enforcement of the United States Fish and Wildlife Service. His job is to catch people who break laws that deal with wildlife, particularly those protecting endangered species. To do it, Rich must sometimes go undercover.

As a wildlife agent, Rich works to stop the illegal selling of endangered species.

"Sometimes I have to pose as a criminal to catch criminals," says Rich. "You have to be something of an actor to work undercover. I guess you have to have a little ham in you."

5

A major part of Rich's work is to stop the trade in illegal wildlife products. The illegal wildlife trade is a big business for criminals around the world. A single rhino horn, for example, can sell for $50,000—and once it is ground up it is worth much, much more. A rare parrot can be worth $40,000.

All told, illegal sales of wildlife are believed to earn criminals $6 billion a year. Sometimes, wildlife criminals also commit other crimes. For example, Rich discovered that "John" was also smuggling machine guns from South Africa and trying to sell them in the United States. Increasingly, gangs that deal in drugs and illegal gambling are also getting into wildlife crime. They think it is a way to make easy money. Rich's task, though, is to make it far from easy and to make them pay for their crimes.

Opposite and at right: Animal products that have been taken from criminals line the walls and tables of Rich's office.

Rich often dresses as a hunter and does "spot checks" to make sure other hunters are obeying the law. Here he checks a hunter's gun for possible violations.

Another part of Rich's job is to make sure that hunting laws are obeyed—such as those limiting the number of waterfowl a hunter can kill. "For example," Rich explains, "the law says that a duck hunter cannot use a shotgun that holds more than three shells. During the duck hunting season, I check hunters' guns to make sure they follow the rules."

When he is out in the field checking on hunters, Rich wears hunting gear and carries a shotgun. "That way anyone who is doing something wrong doesn't realize that I am a special agent until I identify myself."

10

Tracking down wildlife criminals—like any other criminals—can be dangerous. In fact, studies show that wildlife officers are more likely to be killed or injured on the job than any other law enforcement officers.

"Wildlife officers have a risky job because almost everybody they approach is armed," says Assistant United States Attorney James G. Genco, who prosecutes people accused of crimes in Hartford's federal court. "Wildlife officers are often alone in the wilderness and far from help if they need it," Genco explains.

Wildlife agents must often work alone, tracking armed criminals who may be dangerous.

Rich takes a shotgun
out of his firearms
cabinet before going
on an assignment.

With such a job, you might think that Rich is a "James Bond type," but he is not. He is an "average guy," with a wife and two children. For fun, he hunts and fishes and watches sports. He looks as if he might be a salesmen or a business-man. However, when Rich goes to work, he carries a badge, a semi-automatic pistol and, sometimes, a shotgun and a bullet-proof vest.

"Special agents have to carry a pistol on the job," says Rich. "Actually, we are never off duty, although, of course, we get time off. Then, it's up to me whether I carry my gun or not."

Rich works between 50 to 60 hours a week, on the average. When an investigation gets hot, he may put in many more hours than that. His is certainly not a typical 9-to-5 job.

Rich's official badge, which identifies him as a federal agent.

13

The Fish and Wildlife Service has about 200 men and women who are special agents like Rich. Some are stationed in big cities, other are in rural areas. The headquarters of the Fish and Wildlife Service Law Enforcement Division is in Virginia, just outside Washington, D.C. Rich operates his office out of Hartford's Federal Building. He is one of 34 agents in the Service's Northeast Region, which covers an area from Maine to Virginia.

Hartford's Federal Building is headquarters for Rich and the Connecticut office of the Fish and Wildlife Service.

Law enforcement officers, such as local police, often help the Department of Fish and Wildlife in searching for criminal activity.

15

Fish and Wildlife agents sometimes train and work with law enforcement officers in other countries. During his rhino horn investigation, Rich received help from the South African Police because "John" had been getting his illegal wildlife products and machine guns from a crooked officer in the South African Army, named Marius.

"Law enforcement officers from all over the world cooperate in the war against wildlife crime," says Rich. "U.S. Fish and Wildlife agents are respected by all of them."

Customs officers often assist wildlife enforcement by alerting authorities when possible crimes have been committed.

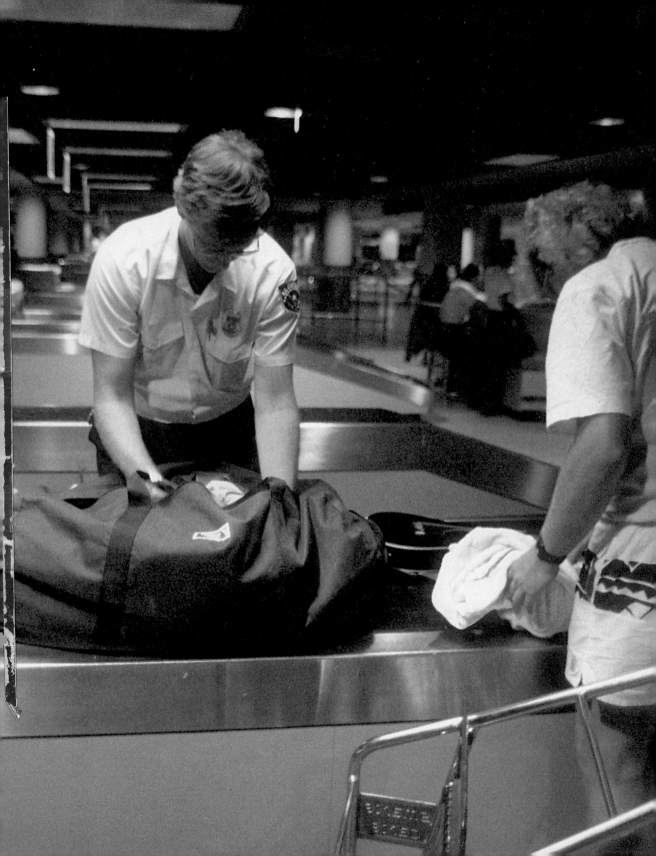

Fish and wildlife agents undergo the same basic training as special agents from many other government agencies. Their basic course takes place at the Federal Law Enforcement Training Center near Brunswick, Georgia. For two months, rookie agents learn how to investigate crime and how the court system works. They are trained in understanding laws, handling firearms, and how to approach crime scenes. They also learn how to guard against terrorism.

"Sometimes people are surprised that wildlife agents are taught to combat terrorism," says Rich. "But we need to know, just in case."

Sometimes Rich's training comes in handy for other assignments. During the 1995 Special Olympics World Games in New Haven, Connecticut, Rich and some of his fellow agents were placed on harbor patrol. Their job was to help security, especially when President Clinton and other important leaders came to the city.

Rookie firearm training for new Fish and Wildlife recruits takes place in Georgia.

After their criminal investigation training, rookies at the Georgia training camp go through a six-week course that is especially designed for Fish and Wildlife Service agents. They learn more about investigating crime, how to raid places such as buildings where criminals have illegal wildlife products, how to use a compass and map, and how to identify wildlife and wildlife parts.

Opposite and at
right: Instructors
at the Georgia
training camp
teach new recruits
about specific
wildlife species
and how to
identify them.

"A Fish and Wildlife agent must be part police officer and
part biologist," says Rich. "Agents must learn to tell if a
crocodile hide is from a protected species or one that can be
legally sold," says Rich.

21

Rich often starts a case because of a tip from a concerned citizen who has discovered that someone is dealing in illegal wildlife. That is how his investigation of "John" began. An honest dealer in wildlife products reports that "John" had asked him if he wanted to buy a mounted leopard. Hunters who legally kill leopards in Africa can bring them back to the United States as trophies. It is illegal, however, to sell them.

If Rich thinks the tip is a good one, he usually tries to make contact with the suspected criminal. Most of the time, he does it undercover. When he telephoned "John," he asked, "Are you the guy who's got the leopard for sale?" "John" said he

Rich often makes contact with suspected smugglers and dealers by posing as a potential buyer.

had already sold it. However, he offered Rich a leopard head for $500. A few days later, "John" called Rich and asked him if he also wanted a leopard rug for $1,200. Rich said he did and met with "John" who sold him the rug and the head.

Next, "John" offered Rich an illegal cheetah rug and head. "John's" contact in the South African Army arranged to have these items smuggled into the United States by air. As he learned more about "John's" operation, Rich talked with agents from the U.S. Customs Service. Their job is to prevent smuggling. So, before long, they were in on the case.

"I get lots of assistance from people in other law enforcement agencies," says Rich. "Sometimes they do it because they have to. Some do it just to help out. U.S. Marshals often help me on raids, often on their own time."

Rich proudly displays one of three rare snow leopard pelts he helped to seize in a recent arrest.

After offering the cheetah rug and head, "John" told Rich he could supply him with a rhino horn. The horn was smuggled into the United States, where "John," in turn, brought it to Connecticut.

The net around John was getting tighter. "He never suspected we were on to him," Rich explains.

When "John" once again flew to Africa, he promised Rich that he would bring back more rhino horns. The trap was about to be sprung. "John" remained in Africa for a couple of weeks, then telephoned Rich. "He told me he would be back on November 2 with a horn," says Rich. "We decided that when he did, we would arrest him."

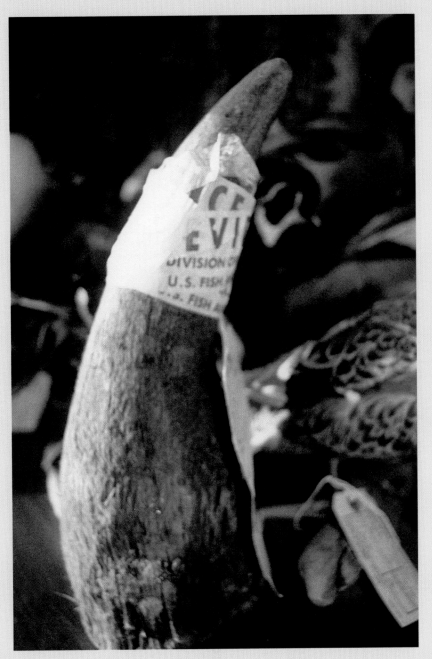

A valuable horn from a black rhino that has been seized as evidence.

27

A person who is arrested by federal agents is brought to the Federal Building, fingerprinted by U.S. Marshals, and then usually held in a cell until presented before a judge in court.

Rich's work on a case is not over once he makes an arrest. "It's really just beginning," says Rich. "For weeks, even months, I have to help the U.S. Attorney organize our evidence. We must plan a strategy for the trial. It takes lots of time and there is a heap of paperwork involved. This is a side of police work that is not at all glamorous. But it is very important. If we don't do it right, someone who is guilty of a crime could go free instead of paying the penalty."

Richard and Assistant U.S. Attorney James Genco go over the strategy for an upcoming trial.

In "John's" case, the penalty was a heavy fine and a jail sentence. "John" publicly apologized for his actions and has not been involved in crime since.

Rich says that he felt sorry for "John," and the others arrested with him. "They weren't hardened criminals," he says. "But they were greedy for money so they turned to crime. When someone commits wildlife crime, it's my job to stop it and bring that person to justice. My personal feelings don't count. What counts is that, for everyone's good, people must live by the law."

Rich's work protects the future of endangered animals not only in North America, but throughout the world.

FURTHER READING

Amos, Janine. *Animals in Danger.* Madison, NJ: Raintree Steck-Vaughn, 1992.

Arnold, Caroline. *Rhino.* New York: Morrow, 1995.

Cuthbert, Susan. *Endangered Creatures.* Elgin, IL: Lion Publishing, 1992.

Stone, Lynn M. *Endangered Animals.* Chicago: Children's Press, 1984.

INDEX